Great Scientific
Questions and the
Scientists Who
Answered Them

HOW DO WE KNOW
THE AGE OF
THE UNIVERSE

MARY LYNN GERMADNIK

Great Scientific Questions and the Scientists Who Answered Them

HOW DO WE KNOW

THE AGE OF THE UNIVERSE

THE ROSEN PUBLISHING GROUP, INC.
NEW YORK

To my family
In loving memory of my grandfather, Albert Germadnik.

Published in 2001 by The Rosen Publishing Group, Inc.
29 East 21st Street, New York, NY 10010

First Edition

Library of Congress Cataloging-in-Publication Data
Germadnik, Mary Lynn, 1967–
How do we know the age of the universe / Mary Lynn Germadnik.—1st ed.
p. cm. — (Great scientific questions and the scientists who answered them)
Includes bibliographical references and index.
ISBN 0-8239-3382-2 (lib. bdg.)
1. Cosmology—Juvenile literature. 2. Astronomers—Biography—Juvenile literature. [1. Astronomers. 2. Cosmology.] I. Title. II. Series.
QB983 .G47 2001
523.1—dc21   2001000783

Cover images: spiral galaxy NGC 1232.
Cover inset: Hubble Space Telescope.

Manufactured in the United States of America

Contents

Introduction

The question is, how old is the universe? For how long has this vast space around us, filled as it is with galaxies and stars and planets and, perhaps, other living beings besides ourselves, been around? For many centuries of human history, this was not a terribly important

The endless, regular movements of the planets convinced early societies that the universe was unchanging.

question. Ancient philosophers and scientists who lived before the twentieth century thought that the universe was a static and an unchanging thing. Sure, there was movement and change in the universe. The planets revolved around the Sun. The physical features of Earth were altered through geological processes. The stars changed position in relation to each other. The universe itself was thought to extend through space infinitely, and it was thought to have existed in its present shape and form for all time. The cosmos was infinite in space and time. It had no beginning or end. The question of its age was meaningless, and it was scientifically unsophisticated to ask.

Scientific discoveries in the twentieth century have overthrown all complacency about the stability of the universe and have left us breathless when we contemplate the true state of things. The universe is neither infinite nor ageless. It is only about 15 billion years old, and far from staying the same, it is evolving. The early universe looked quite different from our universe, and the future universe will look very different as well. To say the universe is evolving is an understatement. It is quite literally exploding. The clusters of galaxies within it rush apart from each other at enormous velocities, while the space between those galaxies expands. How can empty space expand? If we

project backward and reverse this expansion in our minds, can we find the point in space from which everything originated? Will this expansion continue forever, or will gravity pull everything together again at some point in the future? Our universe, like all other things in nature, was born and probably will die. We are, in a sense, parasites living within another larger organism, and its fate is our fate.

What's more, we now know that light, as fast as it is, travels at a finite speed, and light waves travel across the vast distances of the universe. This means that when we look at very distant objects in the universe, we are seeing them as they existed in the past. It has taken billions of years for the light from some very distant galaxies to reach Earth, so that we see those galaxies as they were billions of years ago. What they look like "now," that is, as we are observing them, is something that only astronomers can know, observing billions of years from now. The advantage of this is that the light preserves a historical record of the state of the universe as it existed in the past. When we look across the great distances of the universe, we are also looking back in time. So the question of the age of an expanding universe is connected to how large it is.

The story really begins with Albert Einstein. In 1916, Einstein put forward his general theory of relativity. This was essentially a new theory of gravity. Einstein abandoned Isaac Newton's conception of gravity completely. Einstein said gravity, as a force acting invisibly between two massive objects, did not really exist at all. The underlying reality of the universe was not three-dimensional space but four-dimension space-time. What really happened was that a massive object distorted, or bent, this space-time around itself. Objects traveling through this distorted space-time had to travel in curved paths that gave the illusion that they were influenced by a "force" of gravity. They were merely following curvatures in space-time that were invisible to us.

How could empty space bend? What was the structure within a vacuum that could take different shapes? There was, remember, no such thing as space, only space-time. In the presence of a massive object with a strong gravitational field, time slowed down, and it could be shown that if time slowed down, movement through space happened along curved paths. The space-time of the universe as a whole was curved by the matter within it. This concept of curvature, expressed mathematically as either positive or negative curvature, would determine whether there was enough matter in the universe to stop its expansion.

When Einstein first formulated his general theory of relativity, the equations seemed to demand an unstable universe, one that was either expanding or contracting. After all, time doesn't stand still. We move through time even when we don't move through space. If time was as much a dimension as length or width or depth, the passage of time required movement along some "line." The expansion of space was a feature of the passing of time.

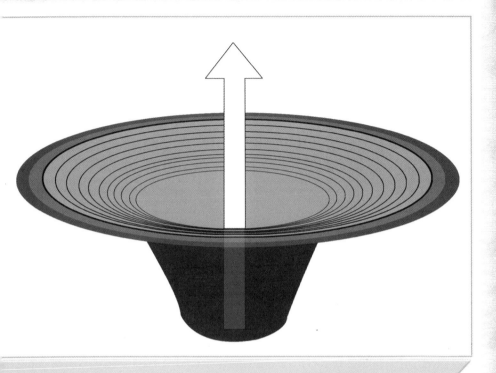

This is a representation of the expansion of space through time.

At the time that he worked out his theory, however, no expansion of space had been measured, and Einstein added a mathematical term, called the "cosmological constant," to his equations in order to keep the universe static and unchanging. He had to discard that constant when the American astronomer Edwin Hubble discovered that the galaxies were, in fact, receding from one another very rapidly. The real universe had caught up with Einstein's relativity theory. This new universe was a very frightening place. It was flying apart in all directions, like shrapnel from a bomb.

This is the story of those scientists who came after Einstein and developed our modern conception of the universe. Here are the people who discovered the expansion of the universe, who explored its distant origins in the violent explosion known as the big bang, who found the evidence of that ancient explosion, and who theorized about both the universe's origin and its ultimate fate. In answering the question about the age of the universe, scientists have been led to explore its nature and origins, and the cosmos has turned out to be a stranger place than anyone had imagined.

Alexander Friedman

1

One of the first individuals to question Einstein's attempt to preserve a static universe was Alexander Friedman (1888–1925). In addition to being a war hero and setting the Soviet record in 1925 for the highest meteorological balloon flight, Alexander Friedman is also credited with

finding Albert Einstein's greatest mathematical error—the cosmological constant—and being the first cosmologist to provide mathematical solutions for an expanding universe. Unfortunately, Friedman died an early, untimely death, unaware of the true significance of his findings in cosmology. His models are used in astronomy and provide the mathematical foundation for most cosmological theories.

Alexander Friedman was born on June 16, 1888 in St. Petersburg, in the western part of Russia. The aspiring mathematician was born into a small Jewish family. Friedman's father was a prominent composer and ballet dancer. Other members of the family were talented musicians. When he was only nine years old, his father, who had earned a reputation for being somewhat cold and overbearing, ended his unhappy marriage with Friedman's mother.

Mr. Friedman convinced the state to grant him custody of Alexander by accusing his ex-wife of marital infidelity. Even though it was actually Friedman's father who had remarried, the church sentenced his mother to celibacy. Friedman's father forbid the boy to see his mother until 1920, when he was considered an adult.

In 1906, Friedman began his academic studies in pure and applied mathematics at St. Petersburg University, where he remained until 1910. Even though he was skilled and had a passion for mathematics, his primary interests were in atmospheric and meteorological physics. In 1913, he took a job as a staff worker at the Aerological Observatory in Pavlovsk where he engrossed himself in weather observations and meteorological science.

During World War I (1914–1918), his career was interrupted when he volunteered to serve in an aviation unit. Initially, he served in the Russian army on the Austrian front. As a technical expert, he worked meticulously on calculations concerning bombs and bomb sites. In a letter, Friedman included detailed calculations on his theory of bomb dropping. He produced equations on the components of bomb

velocity, the acceleration due to gravity, and the effects on its trajectory of the shape and weight of the bomb. He verified his calculations in practice during flights over Przemsyl, an Austrian fortress blockaded by Russian troops. The bombs dropped in the way his theory had anticipated and were responsible for destroying the arsenal inside the fortress. Apparently, he had a reputation for being so highly accurate that whenever a bomb found its target the German soldiers would attribute it to Friedman being in the air. For his air reconnaissance flights over Przemsyl, Friedman received the George Cross for valor on November 23, 1914. Toward the end of the war, he was promoted to officer and was transferred to Kiev, where he was appointed head of the Central Aeronautical Station. He gave lectures on aeronautics at the Kiev school of observer-pilots.

After the war, between 1920 and 1925, Friedman was indefatigable. He took up several impressive positions in Petrograd simultaneously:

He taught mathematics and mechanics at the physics and mathematics faculty of Petrograd University, was professor at the Petrograd Polytechnical Institute, worked as the senior supervisor of studies at the Naval Academy, became a professor at the Institute of Railway Engineering, and carried out research as the acting director of the Geophysical Observatory, an institution of the Academy of Sciences. During these years, he also found time to publish "The World as Space and Time" and the first volume of *Fundamentals of the Theory of Relativity.*

Almost overnight, Friedman went from being a war hero to being one of the forerunners of big bang cosmology. In 1917, Albert Einstein, the father of relativistic cosmology, published a paper entitled "Cosmological Considerations on the General Theory of Relativity" in the *Transactions of the Prussian Academy of Sciences*, an article premiering the newly-formulated general theory of relativity. The theory addressed more than just the properties of gravity.

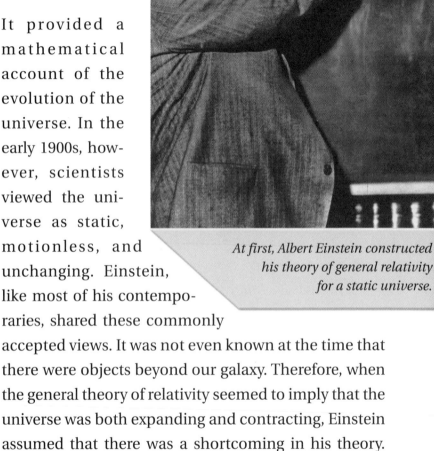

It provided a mathematical account of the evolution of the universe. In the early 1900s, however, scientists viewed the universe as static, motionless, and unchanging. Einstein, like most of his contemporaries, shared these commonly

At first, Albert Einstein constructed his theory of general relativity for a static universe.

accepted views. It was not even known at the time that there were objects beyond our galaxy. Therefore, when the general theory of relativity seemed to imply that the universe was both expanding and contracting, Einstein assumed that there was a shortcoming in his theory. His reaction was to force his equations to support this preconceived notion of a static universe by introducing

When Einstein first announced his theory, all stars were thought to be part of our galaxy.

an arbitrary constant, known as the "cosmological constant," a contrived repulsive force that could counteract gravitational collapse and that could keep the universe in a fixed position.

When Friedman published his work on an evolving cosmological model in 1922, it was the first time anyone had proposed the possibility of a universe in

motion. His paper presented a group of solutions to Einstein's field equations that revealed Einstein's premise of a single static solution to be inadequate. His models, called Friedman universes, were contingent upon whether the curvature of the universe is zero, negative, or positive. This suggested that both closed cyclical and ever-expanding models were possible, depending upon the value given to Einstein's constant. In one situation, the universe might alternately expand and contract forever. In another, gravity was not a strong enough force to cause the universe's expansion to end and reverse itself.

Today, astronomers are using Friedman's models to determine whether the universe will continue to expand forever, suffering a "heat death" when all energy is uniformly distributed, or whether it will contract back on itself into what is known as the big crunch. Not enough is known about the amount of matter in the universe to answer this question definitively. Recent observations suggest that at great distances the galaxies are moving away from us even more rapidly and that gravity is not slowing down the expansion of the universe.

Friedman's article, "The World as Space and Time," was published in the distinguished journal of physics *Zeitschrift für Physik* and in the *Astronomischer Jahresbericht*, a leading journal in astronomy. Yet Friedman's work was ignored by his contemporaries. Refusing to acknowledge Friedman's model, Einstein claimed that he had made no mathematical errors. Eventually, Einstein was persuaded by Yuri Krutkov, another Russian physicist, who was both a friend and colleague of Friedman, to further consider Friedman's paper. Reluctantly, Einstein later agreed with Friedman, admitting publicly that he had made a mathematical oversight in his calculations. Yet even as he validated and accepted Friedman's evolutionary solutions in a mathematical sense, he initially did not believe that they had bearing on the structure of the real universe. At the time, Friedman did not necessarily believe in an

expanding model and was not concerned with whether his models had any bearing on the physical nature of the real universe. He was interested only in having the mathematical importance of his models recognized by Einstein. It was not until several years later, after the observation of expanding space was reported, that Einstein realized the extent of his error and announced the inclusion of the constant to be a mistake, calling it "the biggest blunder of my life."

Alexander Friedman died in 1925 at the age of thirty-seven, unaware that in only four short years the solution present in his model for an expanding universe would be observed through the 100-inch Hooker telescope at Mount Wilson Observatory by Edwin Hubble and Milton Humason. The exact cause of his untimely death still remains a mystery. Although his doctors and colleagues claimed his death to be the result of typhoid fever, cosmologist George Gamow, who was one of Friedman's pupils, thought that the obscure illness was really a bout of pneumonia

Astronomer Edwin Hubble studied distant receding galaxies and concluded that the universe is expanding.

brought on by his last high altitude balloon excursion, where he reached a Soviet record altitude of 7,400 meters.

Friedman's belief that Einstein's theories prohibited a static universe would be confirmed by Edwin Hubble.

Edwin Hubble

Edwin Hubble (1889–1953) was an Oxford trained attorney and a professional boxer who later became an American astronomer and cosmologist. Hubble is credited with two of the most important contributions in the study of the size and age of the universe. First, by measuring the distance to the stars beyond our solar system, he discovered that other galaxies existed beyond the Milky Way. He extended the outer boundary of the universe by 500,000 million light years. Then, with the help of Milton Humason, Hubble realized that light from distant galaxies was redshifted, or at a lower requency than it should have been, and that the galaxies therefore were moving away from one another at a velocity proportional to their distance. That is, the farther away they were, the faster they were receding. From this it has been surmised that it is not the galaxies that are actually moving, but the space between them that is stretching and expanding. As a result, Hubble's observations supported Friedman's earlier mathematical predictions—that we are living in an expanding universe.

Hubble was born on November 20, 1889, in Marshfield, Missouri. In 1910, he received a bachelor of science degree from the University of Chicago. He was a natural athlete and was offered a chance at now attenuated, or stretched out, into low energy radio waves. Gamow had predicted in 1948 that this relic radiation should be detectable. It was not until Penzias and Wilson found this residual radiation that Gamow's theory was seriously considered. Scientists who once referred to the big bang theory as pure speculation began to look at Gamow's theory and accept it as "the standard model" for the origin of the universe.

Arno Penzias was born into a Jewish family on April 26, 1933, in Munich, Germany. In 1939, his parents fled from Nazi Germany to England, and later that year immigrated with their children to New York City, where they became naturalized citizens of the United States. In 1954, Penzias earned a bachelor's degree in physics from City College of New York, and he continued his education at Columbia University as a graduate student, where he received both master's and doctorate degrees by 1962.

Robert Woodrow Wilson was born on January 10, 1936, in Houston, Texas. His father was a chemical engineer who worked in the oil industry. He came from a

family that valued a good education, and he was known to have been an extraordinary student. After obtaining a bachelor's at Rice University in 1957, he went on to graduate with a master's degree in chemistry. He was granted a doctorate in 1962 for his research at the California Institute of Technology. He was appointed head of the radio-physics department in 1976.

Penzias and Wilson made their discovery accidentally while they were working at Bell Labs in Crawford Hill, New Jersey, calibrating an elaborate but small twenty-foot directional radio telescope. The horn-shaped reflector was the first antenna in the world capable of trapping high-frequency, short radio waves—known as microwaves. It had been designed to detect radio emissions from the Echo satellite. Being unfamiliar with Gamow's ideas at the time, the two men were not looking for microwave background radiation encircling the universe, but instead were collaborating on a project designed to identify and eliminate all other forms of radio emission that might garble the radio signal for which they were looking. Specifically, they were trying to study the characteristics of radio emissions from the halo—a ring of gas—surrounding the Milky Way, our galaxy.

The two young engineers made a series of observations with their radio telescope. They were bewildered as their antenna continued to pick up a faint but persistent background "noise," like radio static. Regardless of where they pointed the microwave antenna in the sky, they detected the same background radiation. The radio emission was a uniform signal arriving from all directions in the sky. It had been assumed, prior to Gamow's work, that empty space had a temperature of absolute zero. There should not have been any thermal radiation from deep space.

Embarrassed and fearing that they were making a mistake, Penzias and Wilson worked frantically to locate all possible sources of interference in order to rule them out. As long as the noise continued, the antenna remained unusable for astronomical research

involving highly sensitive measurements. They checked their surroundings for a ground-based source of static. They examined the amplifier that they were using, and even the antenna, checking it for bird droppings. They cleared away all the pigeon droppings from their instrument, took it apart, cleaned it, and then secured all the rivets with aluminum fixtures, hoping that this would eliminate the hidden source of interference. Because the noise was the same in all directions, they were able to eliminate the possibility of terrestrial interference from another radio transmitter or static from some electrical device. They also understood that what they were measuring could not be solar in origin or from the Milky Way. The source of emission was not the Sun, or the disk of our galaxy—the source appeared to be omnidirectional. It was present whether the Sun was in the sky or not. Much to their dismay, after months of repeatedly checking their equipment for all possible sources of error, they were still unable to determine the cause of the signal—the origin of this

strange "excessive noise." Believing their research project was doomed, the two scientists planned to bury their results in the middle of a long scientific paper.

Penzias and Wilson took their results to Robert Dicke (1916–), a professor of physics at Princeton University. Dicke was famous for the scalar-tensor field theory, one of the most scientifically solid alternatives to Einstein's general theory of relativity. Experiments have not yet been devised that can determine whether Einstein or Dicke has the better theory. Dicke was already theorizing about remnant radiation thought to be left over from the big bang. Dicke had estimated a temperature of 3° Kelvin for this radiation, in agreement with the results of the observations made by Penzias and Wilson.

Penzias and Wilson were globally recognized for what is considered to be the most significant discovery in modern radio astronomy. For their detection of the background radiation, they were jointly honored with the Nobel Prize in physics in 1978. They also received both the Herschel Award from the Royal Astronomical Society and the Henry Draper Medal of the National Academy of Sciences.

Penzias and Wilson also demonstrated that there was useful information about the universe that

Robert Dicke convinced Penzias and Wilson that they had indeed detected the cosmic microwave background.

could be obtained from methods other than optical astronomy. The universe was radiating energy all across the electromagnetic spectrum, as radio waves, infrared and ultraviolet waves, X rays, and gamma rays. Many of these emissions cannot be detected on Earth because the atmosphere blocks their transmission, but in the age of artificial satellites it is possible to

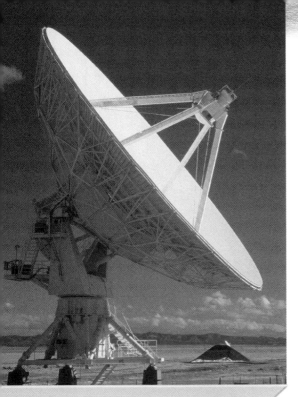

Radio telescopes operate day and night and do not require either a dark or clear sky.

put a detection device above the atmosphere to record this radiation. Radio telescopes, on the other hand, can operate day and night. Unlike optical telescopes, they do not require a dark sky for viewing.

Penzias and Wilson ushered in a new era of radio astronomy that would lead to a conception of the universe as more active and violent than anyone had imagined. It is principally through radio astronomy, or the coordination of radio telescope observations with optical observations, that we have explored such exotic objects as pulsars, black holes, quasars, and other celestial bodies that emit large amounts of

The Pulsar Lighthouse Effect

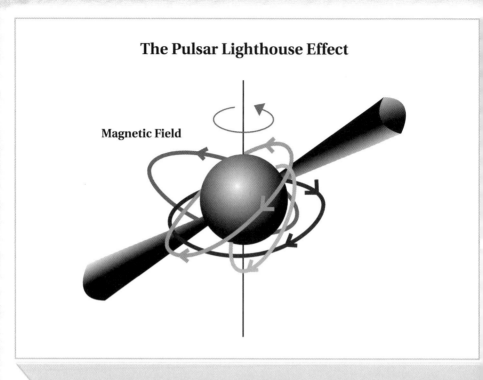

Magnetic Field

Pulsars appear to pulse, or flash on and off, because the magnetic field focuses its radiation into two cones of light that rotate rapidly past the observer.

radiation at radio wavelengths. Some of these celestial objects may be invisible through optical telescopes, but when they are viewed through radio telescopes or with the aid of satellites that can detect X rays or gamma rays, many of these objects appear to be undergoing violent physical processes. There is a lot more to the universe than what we can see with our eyes.

ARNO PENZIAS AND ROBERT WILSON

Some of the exotic objects in the universe, black holes in particular, have led physicists to speculate about the unusual conditions that existed in the early universe. One of those whose speculations have aroused great interest is British physicist Stephen Hawking.

Stephen Hawking

British theoretical physicist Stephen Hawking was born in Oxford, England, on January 8, 1942, on the 300th anniversary of Galileo Galilei's death. Hawking is recognized for his research on black holes. Using Einstein's general theory of relativity, Stephen Hawking and Roger Penrose showed that the effects of gravitation make black holes unavoidable. They predicted that, because massive collapsing stars eventually end in black holes, there is a chance that the violent conditions during the big bang created a series of "mini-black holes" now spread across the universe.

From a very young age, Hawking's life was unpredictable and full of incident. He was born during the upheaval of World War II. During the war, it was considered safer to raise children outside of London and away from the German bombings, so his parents moved to Oxford to give birth to Stephen. However, after Stephen was born, his mother took him back to their house in London. When Stephen was only two years old, the Hawkings were fortunate in being away from home when a V-2 rocket damaged their London residence and destroyed a house next door.

In 1950, his parents moved the family to Saint Albans. Frank and Isobel Hawking were well-educated English intellectuals. Stephen's father, a physician and disease specialist, often traveled to Africa to further his

Stephen Hawking

medical research. Stephen's mother took care of the children, and, as a member of the Liberal Party, stayed politically active. The home of the eccentric couple was scattered with books and old artifacts, and a London taxi served as the family car. Eventually, the taxi was traded in for a green Ford Consul, which they drove to India and back on a yearlong family vacation.

Hawking proved to be an unusual and interesting person. As a schoolboy, he attended Saint Albans private school—from which he received a scholarship for his stellar academics, even though he rarely ever had to study. Because he had a somewhat lanky and awkward frame, Hawking was not equipped for most athletics, but he did have a natural ability at cross-country running and later enjoyed boat racing. In his spare time, he was known to build model aircraft, devise military and political board games, and tinker with electronic gadgets. Once, with the help of his friends, Hawking even built a computerized calculating machine for a class project. Even though it would seem like an unwieldy dinosaur compared to the machines of modern times, this was quite a feat in the 1950s.

In 1962, Hawking received his bachelor's degree in mathematics and physics with honors from University College at Oxford. By the remarkably young age of thirty-three, he was named a fellow of the Royal Society and had earned a doctorate from the Department of Applied Mathematics and Theoretical Physics at Cambridge University. In 1978, he received the Albert Einstein Award, one of the most prestigious prizes in theoretical physics. He was inaugurated

Lucasian professor of mathematics at Cambridge University in 1979, a post once held by Isaac Newton.

Hawking's life was also filled with tragedy. While studying at Oxford, he had growing difficulty with coordination. His speech began to slur, he had difficulty tying his shoes, and he even fell over a few times without apparent cause. During his first year at Cambridge, the same year that he began studying relativity and cosmology, he was diagnosed with an incurable disease known as amyotrophic lateral sclerosis (ALS). This is a type of multiple sclerosis, known in the United States as Lou Gehrig's disease, named after the famous Yankee baseball player who was stricken by the disease in 1939.

ALS progressively weakens the muscles of the body and eventually causes death. It does not affect intellectual function. Therefore Hawking was able to go on with his career studying theoretical physics. At the young age of twenty-one, Hawking's doctors gave him only a few years to live. Hawking, now fifty-nine, seems to have beaten the odds, but has suffered many set-backs with increasing physical limitations. Over time, he became progressively incapacitated and was eventually restricted to a wheelchair because of spinal paralysis. Then in 1985, as a result of a bout of pneumonia, Hawking was forced to have a tracheotomy operation, during which a breathing mechanism was implanted in his windpipe. This resulted in the complete loss of his vocal cords and left him unable to speak with family and colleagues.

Fortunately, Hawking was soon able to communicate with others when computer wizard Walt Woltosz from California found out about Hawking's dilemma and devised a computerized speaking device for him. Using this system, Hawking could choose up to ten words a minute from a series of menus. Later, David Mason equipped him with a small computer and voice synthesizer, which is mounted directly onto his wheelchair. He could then manage up to fifteen words a minute. The handheld switch, sensitive to pressure from

This is an artist's illustration of the accretion disk of gas and dust that surrounds a black hole.

his fingertips, allows him to select words on a computer screen. These words are then combined into sentences, which are conveyed as audible words through a voice synthesizer, called Speech Plus. This program has also enabled him to give lectures and presentations, with the only drawback being that Hawking is British and the synthesizer gives him an American accent.

Hawking's work has been primarily with black holes and the relationship between general relativity and quantum physics. General relativity predicts the existence of black holes, massive stars that collapse and shrink to such density that even light cannot overcome their gravity. The matter within these black holes is said to exist in a degenerate state. Whatever it is, it is not composed of regular atoms or even sub-atomic particles like protons and neutrons, because such particles are destroyed by the intense gravitational field. In fact, within a black hole, theoretically, all particles are crushed to a single mathematical point. We have no understanding of what such a state of matter might be like, or what laws of physics apply when so much mass is crushed into an infinitesimally small space. Quantum physics predicts that matter can escape from black holes and that smaller black holes are likely to "evaporate" over time. When these smaller black holes evaporate, they leave behind a burst of gamma radiation that should be detectable.

The question of whether or not such mini black holes exist has not yet been decided.

Hawking is searching for the grand "theory of everything." Scientists hope that quantum theory, which deals with the inner workings of atoms, can be united with general relativity into one unified theory that would provide a coherent explanation for all the forces of nature. Einstein searched for a grand unified theory during the last decades of his life, and the answer eluded him. The relationship between gravity and the other forces of nature, electromagnetism and the forces within the nucleus of the atom, has yet to be discovered. Physicists believe that they have established a connection between electromagnetism and the two forces within the atom, the strong and weak nuclear forces, but how gravity relates to these forces is elusive. There is no requirement in nature that all of these forces be related, but scientists would find it very satisfying if they could demonstrate that all the phenomena in the universe are explained by one fundamental relationship of forces.

We know that the universe is about 14 or 15 billion years old and is still in the process of evolving. The question of whether it will continue to expand forever or contract into another superdense object and then explode into a new universe is not at present answerable. In spite of recent evidence that the universe appears to be expanding at an increasing rate, many astronomers are still searching for the "missing mass," the matter that would make the universe dense enough for gravity to pull everything together again. We are at the very cutting edge of knowing, but the answer may have to wait for more powerful telescopes. If past experience is any guide, those new instruments may expose us to even more bizarre facts about our universe, and our puzzlement may know no end.

Glossary

big bang theory A cosmological model of the universe, which states that the universe began as an extremely dense, hot superatom containing all the mass in the cosmos, that exploded to create the universe approximately 12 to 15 billion years ago.

black hole A massive object, usually a collapsed star, whose gravitational pull is so intense that it prevents all matter and light from escaping.

Cepheid variable A pulsating star whose brightness waxes and wanes over a period of days or weeks. The absolute brightness attained by a Cepheid variable is always related to its period, the length of time it takes to brighten. If you know the period of such a star, you know its intrinsic brightness and can estimate its distance from Earth.

cosmic microwave background radiation Residual radiation in the range of microwaves, equivalent to a temperature of 3° Kelvin, which has traveled through the universe ever since the big bang.

cosmological constant A number representing a theorized repulsive force, the opposite of gravitational attraction, which Einstein introduced into the general theory of relativity so that he could maintain a static universe.

cosmology The science that studies the evolution, origin, and large-scale structure of the universe.

critical density The average density of the entire
universe, which will determine whether the
universe continues to expand forever or
whether it will stop expanding and begin
to contract.

dark matter Invisible matter that does not
emit light, but can be detected by its
gravitational effects on the motion of
stars and gases.

Friedman model A model dependent on the
curvature of space that will either be
positive, negative, or zero.

galaxy A cluster of 10 million to 10 trillion stars
held together by gravitational force. Our
galaxy is often referred to as the Milky
Way galaxy.

Hubble's law A mathematical expression that
states that the more distant a galaxy is,
the faster it will recede from Earth.

nebula   A cloud of interstellar gas and dust. Before their true nature was understood, galaxies were also called nebulae.

radio astronomy   The branch of astronomy that studies radio waves emitted from celestial bodies.

radio telescope   A device that detects radio waves given off by astronomical bodies.

redshift   The lengthened wavelengths of light emitted by a star moving away from Earth.

singularity   An object so massive that its gravitational pull prevents all matter and light from escaping, so that no information can be obtained about what is happening within it.

steady-state theory   A cosmological theory developed by Bondi, Gold, and Hoyle. It states that the universe has always been the same as it is

today and is not expanding as a result of a massive explosion in the distant past.

general theory of relativity   Theory of gravitation developed by Albert Einstein. According to this theory, gravity is an effect of the curvature of the space-time continuum.

wavelength   The distance between two adjacent peaks or troughs of a wave.

For More Information

WEB SITES

Albert Einstein Archives
http://sites.huji.ac.il/jnul/einstein

Albert Einstein Home Page
http://www.humboldt1.com/~gralsto/einstein/
　　einstein.html

Alexander Friedmann
http://spaceboy.nasda.go.jp/note/kagaku/E/
　　kag110_friedmann_e.html

Arno Penzias/Nobel Prize
http://www.bell-labs.com/user/apenzias/nobel.html

Astronomy Café
http://www.theastronomycafe.net

The Cosmic Microwave Background Radiation
http://cfpa.berkeley.edu/darkmat/cmb.html

Cosmic Microwave Background Radiation
http://map.gsfc.nasa.gov/html/cbr.html

Einstein Revealed
http://www.pbs.org/wgbh/nova/einstein

Eric's Treasure Trove of Astronomy
http://www.treasure-troves.com/astro

FAQs in Cosmology
http://www.astro.ucla.edu/~wright/
            cosmology_faq.html

FOR MORE INFORMATION

Fred Hoyle
http://spaceboy.nasda.go.jp/Note/Kagaku/E/
      kag122_hoyle_e.html

Galaxy Astronomy
http://galaxy.tradewave.com/galaxy/Science/
      Astronomy.html

The Galaxy Page
http://www.seds.org/galaxy

Hubble Constant
http://www.hubbleconstant.com

The Life of George Gamow
http://spot.colorado.edu/~gamow/george/
      prof_life.html

Live From the Hubble Space Telescope
http://quest.arc.nasa.gov/hst/about/
      edwin.html

Origin and Destiny of The Universe
http://imagine.gsfc.nasa.gov/docs/
    introduction/origin_destiny.html

Roger Penrose, Gravitational Physics
http://www.phys.psu.edu/faculty/PenroseR

A Science Odyssey: People and Discoveries:
    Edwin Hubble
http://www.pbs.org/wgbh/aso/databank/
    entries/bahubb.html

Stephen Hawking Official Homepage
http://www.hawking.org.uk

Stephen Hawking's Universe
http://www.pbs.org/wnet/hawking/html/home.html

for further Reading

Consolmagno, Guy J., and Dan M. Davis. *Turn Left at Orion: A Hundred Night Sky Objects to See in a Small Telescope and How to Find Them.* New York: Cambridge University Press, 2000.

Dickinson, Terence. *NightWatch: A Practical Guide to Viewing the Universe.* Willowdale, Ontario: Firefly Books Ltd., 1998.

Dickinson, Terence. *The Universe and Beyond.* Willowdale, Ontario: Firefly Books Ltd., 1999

Forey, Pamela, Cecilia Fitzsimons, and Ian Ridpath. *An Instant Guide to Stars and Planets: The Sky at Night Described and Illustrated in Full Color.* New York: Random House, Inc., 1988.

Vanin, Gabrielle. *A Photographic Tour of the Universe.* Willowdale, Ontario: Firefly Books Ltd., 1999.

Voit, Mark. *Hubble Space Telescope: New Views of the Universe.* New York: Harry N. Abrams, Inc., 2000.

Wilson, Lynn. *What's Out There? A Book About Space* New York: Grosset & Dunlap, 1993.

Index

Credits

ABOUT THE AUTHOR

Mary Lynn Germadnik is a freelance science writer based in Boulder, Colorado. She was born in 1967 in Sharpsville, Pennsylvania. Currently, she is a student at the University of Colorado, Boulder, where she is enrolled in an interdisciplinary BA/MA Program in cognitive science. She is working on an honor's thesis and completing work for certificates in both computer science and neuroscience.

ACKNOWLEDGMENTS

The author would like to thank Cindy Umholtz for all her support in typing and editing this manuscript. She would also like to thank Dr. Nan Goodman and Georgeann Rettburg for teaching her that writing is a process.

PHOTO CREDITS

Cover © European Southern Observatory; cover inset © Space Telescope Science Institute; p. 8 © DigitalVision; pp. 20, 28, 62 © AP/Wide World; p. 21 © Hubble Heritage Team (AUEA/STScI/NASA); pp. 25, 33, 40, 52, 60, 82 © Bettmann/Corbis; pp. 30, 47, 76 © Roger Ressmeyer/Corbis; pp. 32, 63 © Corbis; p. 34 © National Optical Astronomy Observatories; p. 41 © Hulton Getty Archive/Liaison; p. 44 © W. N. Colley, E. Turner, J. A. Tyson, and NASA; p. 53 © E. Schrempp/Photo Researchers; p. 54 © Hulton/Archive; p. 68 © Hulton-Deutsch Collection/Corbis; p. 71 © Hubble Space Telescope; p. 83 © E.J. West/Index Stock Imagery; p. 88 © Michael S. Yamashita/Corbis; p. 92 © John Foster/Photo Researchers. Diagrams on pp. 13, 84 by Geri Giordano.

DESIGN AND LAYOUT

Evelyn Horovicz